I0670171

Award-Winning Essays

Award-Winning Essays

2015

Miglior Press Essay Contest

MIGLIOR PRESS

ATHENS, GEORGIA

Published by Miglior Press
Athens, Georgia
www.migliorpress.com

Cover design by The Adsmith.

The text of this book is set in
ITC Legacy Serif, designed by Ronald Arnholm.

ISBN 978-0-9836484-5-1

Printed in the United States of America

Contents

Foreword

This contest began with an essay. The essay began when I felt compelled to develop it after an experience that seemed certain to be recounted to close friends and family and reiterated for the sake of personal memory. In fear of proving once again the truth of Hemingway's "talking kills writing," I quietly allowed the experience to marinate, so to speak, for a while. After I got around to writing the essay, I sent it to the aforementioned friends and family. And that might have been the end of it.

However, as fate would have it, a friend passed along a copy of a popular magazine that was sponsoring an essay contest with a theme that the above-noted essay addressed. After some more editing, off it went. While the essay did not rise above the rest, the experience did plant a seed: our press could sponsor an essay contest.

Essays have long been important to us. We are "plugged in," of course, and spend a lot of time reading screens, but we remain devoted to the printed word—to books, magazines, newspapers, nutrition labels, flyers, whatever print presents itself to us. Part of what drove our desire to underwrite this contest was the idea of offering another possibility to writers for a physical place for their work, a book to give to those who support them, care about them, something to hand to Grandma or to a prospective publisher, include with a conference-session proposal, cite on a résumé. Something that might, perhaps, open a door.

We left the topic and length up to the writer, as we will continue to do for the foreseeable future. It is fun to see what people want to write about, what sort of possibilities appear.

For our first contest anthology, we have an interesting geographical sweep regarding the settings of the various essays: India; Jupiter; Boston; Athens and Wilkes County, Georgia; and Laos. And we have, it seems, at least four generations of writers represented. The collection, universal and personal at the same time, will take you not just from India to Laos, but from Pasteur and the Dalai Lama to labyrinths and loss, from assault and reparations to a contemplative journey home, and then back in time to the Plain of Jars.

We thank all who entered, and congratulate the first-prize winner, Matthew Chabin, and the four finalists: Sara Amis, Sara T. Baker, Cecilia Walker, and Ben B. Walton.

Donna Maddock-Cowart
Miglior Press

First-Place Winner

Matthew Chabin

The Dogs of Dharamsala

Matthew Chabin

When I was a kid I used to dream about rabid dogs. Bad dreams (need I say?). Classics. Even now, many a-nightmare down the road, the Rabid Dog dreams of my early youth rank among the worst.

I'd be in a public place, typically, a playground, or a mall, or the parking lot outside my school. There'd be a dog somewhere. A goddamn dog. Not conspicuous at first, just trotting along in the background, but sooner or later I'd notice the dog acting strange. Looking at me. Shaking its head. *Smiling.* Everyone knows smiling dogs are bad news. Sometimes I'd run, and sometimes I'd be too petrified with fear. Usually I'd wake up before the biting started, but at least once I did not. I remember the sensation of deep, tingling pressure on my arm, the dreamdog sinking its infectious dreamteeth with crazed, googly-eyed triumph.

Now here I was, some thirty years later, a bag full of raw meat and syringes on my shoulder, chasing dogs through a maze of narrow corridors in the Dalai Lama's temple complex. It seemed the tables had turned. This—would you believe it?—was no dream.

So why rabid dogs? That stupid book had a lot to do with it. Some well-intentioned soul had written an illustrated children's book called *The Importance of Believing in Yourself*, about

3

Louis Pasteur and his quest for a rabies vaccine. (I remember the little antibody soldiers marching in ranks against the squiggly, malevolent germs.) The story goes like this. A little boy is bitten by a rabid dog and will surely die, but Pasteur, practicing without a license, tries his experimental vaccine and cures him. It's a story about rationalism and home-brewed gumption overcoming ignorance and death, and not for nothing. Before Pasteur came along, hardly anyone believed in germs, and the list of traditional rabies treatments reads like one of Steve Martin's "Medieval Barber" sketches.

"Perhaps if we cut the membrane that attaches the tongue, we can get at the worm that lives there."

"Perhaps. Have you tried a mercury enema yet?"

"We should purify the wound with the Key of Saint Hubert!"

"Naturally. Boy, fetch the key from the fire."

So, yes, three big cheers for Dr. Pasteur and progress. Still, one can imagine how this little fable strikes the ears of first graders.

Hey, kids, you know that disease that makes friendly neighborhood dogs go crazy and bite little children, so they get sick and scared of water, and their brains swell up, and they die? Well—really, first you've heard of it? Well, guess what? There's a cure! Oh . . . . Bunch of shots in the stomach with an 8-gauge bore needle. Sure it hurts, but you know what hurts worse than the cure? The disease! Say it with me kids.

Rabies!

Rabies, yeah, from the Latin for "rage," Greek *lyssa* ("madness"). On its face, the idea of going crazy had its charms back then; no bed times for crazy people, right? But on some level I must have also grasped the real horror of insanity, the possibility that the world I was just learning to paste together could suddenly fly to pieces because a goddamn dog bit me. Just the idea of a mad dog, something friendly and cute turned ferocious and cruel, a monster grinning through the happy masks of childhood—that (I believe now) was what the dreams were really about. And that was what made a children's book scarier than a whole closet full of certified boogeymen.

But that was then, some thirty years ago. And I wasn't a scared little kid anymore.

The opening ceremonies of World Rabies Day took place on the broad, sun-warmed deck of the Tibet Charity School where I'd been teaching for the last four months. There were thirty or forty students, plus teachers, administrators, nursing and veterinary corps, and a visiting official from the Department of Animal Husbandry. Also a good many local Tibetans who'd brought in dogs to be vaccinated. The atmosphere was mildly festive.

The government official, speaking in Hindi to a mostly Tibetan audience, sounded terse. I found out later that he was annoyed that this observance was more than a week overdue, as if anything in India happens on schedule. The Tibetans had their reasons for the postponement; they'd been occupied with ceremonies and councils following a spike in self-immolation protests in the homeland—people lighting themselves on fire, forty that year alone—but either the guy didn't know this or didn't think it important enough to muck with the calendar. To be fair, obliviousness ran both ways; I heard later that some of the students thought it was "Dog Celebration Day."

The speeches done, it was time to vaccinate the first dog. Tashi, the venerable ivory-yellow alpha governor of lower Temple Road, was led into the center of the courtyard. The director of the school gave him a treat and doted on his big, placid head while the government man slipped the needle into the skin of his rump. Tashi gave a low growl and everyone applauded.

The locals who had brought their dogs then formed a line, and the veterinary team spread out to give the shots. Each dog received a treat, a shot, and a dab of red paint atop the head where they couldn't lick it off, rather like the *talika* marks of the Hindus. I thought I recognized one of the green-shirted men giving the shots, though he looked different out of his monk's robes.

"Excuse me, you're Thukjay?"

His round, genial face smiled up at me. "Yes, that's me."

"You're the head of the Animal Welfare Department?" He beamed again. "Rinzin said maybe you could use a hand with the vaccinations today. My classes were canceled because of Rabies Day, so I thought . . . ."

"You want to help give the shots?"

"Sure."

"Okay," he said. "Watch how I do it."

It takes a sure, quick hand to give a shot to something that can turn around and bite you, but Thukjay had it down. I watched as he fed the pink serum under the hide of a small, dappled mutt, who showed no sign of feeling it. "Not so difficult," he said. "The best thing is to distract them." I nodded. "You'll need a green shirt. I think Jamba has them."

The team consisted of four Tibetans—Thukjay, Jamba, a woman named Tsering, and Dolma, the building supervisor who'd once given me a ride on his motorcycle in a monsoon downpour from Dharmakot to Dharamsala. There was also an Indian man who introduced himself as Vishnu.

"Vishnu," I said, "like the god."

"Yes," he said, embarrassed, "but I am not a god."

I thought of pointing out that according to certain schools of Vedanta we are all "god," that is, Brahman. Then thought better of lecturing the god Vishnu on Hinduism.

Even this late in the year, even at this altitude, India is hot, and chasing dogs up and down the gullies and hills proved thirsty work. The gang of delinquent mongrels that hung around the top of Temple Road watched us as we made the climb, and waited until we started calling them before retreating into the vast complex of the Tsuglag Khang, where His Holiness the Dalai Lama lives and teaches. Refuge in the temple—an old trick. Little did they know the Dalai Lama had sent us, in a manner of speaking, having started the program with funds from the Bridget Bardot Foundation some years back.

Past the enormous harlequin cow who hangs around the entrance, past the giant poster showing the faces of the immolated martyrs, up the stairs and through the Nyamgal Gompa, the long, covered hall where the monks hold their raucous floor debates. It was good to be out of the sun, but we found the dogs had slipped our pursuit. We were about to turn back when an old, grinning monk emerged from a stairway and waved us further in, towards the living quarters where visitors rarely tread.

Up more stairs, and along a balcony walkway overlooking a courtyard—here we spotted one of our quarry, a thin, pale rumor of a beast, as she turned down an interior corridor. We found her there, cornered, dolorous, little panting ghost-girl mantled in shade. I dropped a piece of meat. She whined. I cooed to her and kissed the air. Vishnu tried to move closer, but she shied and paced nimbly between us. Behind us, several monks had stepped out to watch the show.

She was too spooked to come quietly, so we called down for one of the catch poles. Vishnu got the noose around her neck without difficulty, but as soon as he tried to pin her, she flew into a wild panic, twisting and thrashing at the end of the pole, her cries ringing off the walls. Finally, he had to release her for fear she would strangle herself. She shot past my legs and was gone.

Down in the courtyard we could see that Thukjay and Jamba were having more luck, coaxing a hobbled and blind old black-and-tan to accept a treat. Thukjay moved in, scrubbing the lower back with his knuckles and plucking the hide and slipping the needle. The dog whined and limped away, but not before Jamba touched its head with the paintbrush—there! In a moment even the one that got away from us was made safer, buffered by the mathematics of herd immunity against the tide of madness and death.

Science! Reason! Enlightenment!

We certainly had our work cut out for us.

Rabies, from the Latin *rabbis* ("rage"), related to the Sanskrit *rabhas* ("to do violence"), has long history in India. It's mentioned in the Vedas, and Yama, the Hindu god of death—the same who challenged the Buddha at the threshold of his awakening—is preceded in the world by his messengers, a pair of raging, four-eyed, brindled curs. But to understand the problem in all its modern ramifications takes a bit of study. For a visual, consider this little mobile of karmic correlative that hangs over every child born to the subcontinent:

?
Sky Burials
Compassion for Animals
RELIGION
Ignorance/Superstition
Vultures
Puppy Pregnancy Syndrome
DOGS
RABIES

Diclofenac
Successful Vaccination Program
MODERN MEDICINE

Hard to know where to begin, but we'll follow the first rule of heuristics in India: when in doubt, start with the cows.

The exact role of the cow in Hindu religion remains somewhat vague, partly because Hinduism itself is a patchwork of diverse, overlapping, and sometimes contradictory doctrines and practices. Cows are not, as is commonly thought, worshiped as proxy gods, nor are they reviled as taboo animals the way pigs are by Muslims and Jews. Rather, their status seems to fall somewhere in between. At various times they have been treated as food, as sacrificial victims and totem animals, as pastoral commodities, as allegorical religious symbols, and even as political causes. To those who preach that the sacred status of cows is a myth, an invention of orientalizing Westerners, it should be noted that cows are consistently associated with divinity in India, especially with Shiva and the Brahman priesthood, and that no less a Hindu than Gandhi made cow veneration a key part of his propaganda campaign against the markedly carnivorous Raj. And yet I have seen a rural woman beat a pestering cow from her doorway and throw the switch after it as it ran. Veneration apparently has its limits.

In any case, the well-meaning Hindu of today faces a dilemma when these hapless animals fall into decrepitude. Can't kill them. Let them languish? In the 1990s the practice of dosing them with modern veterinary painkillers gained traction, and if the incidence of rabid dog attacks began to tick up shortly thereafter, no one drew an immediate connection. Why would they?

The Parsis might have been the first to notice something was amiss. A community of latter-day Zoroastrians centered near Mumbai, Parsis venerate the three elements of earth, fire, and water, and therefore must refrain from polluting these elements with their dead. They practice "sky burials," exposing the departed on *dakhmas*, "towers of silence," large, open ossuaries where the bodies are consumed by vultures. But whereas a healthy convocation of the birds can devour a body in just under half an hour, at the start of the new millennium the process was found to be taking weeks. What had been one of the most efficient and ecologically sound funerary practices anywhere became, in short order, a foul backlog of decomposing flesh.

The culprit, it turned out, was an anti-inflammatory/analgesic drug called diclofenac. The Hindus were giving it to the cows to ease their pain, and the vultures that fed on the cows, vultures whose acidic stomachs are dead-end terminals for everything from rabies to bubonic plague, lacked the particular enzyme needed to process the drug. This led to renal failure and death on a massive scale—99.9% in the case of India's white-rumped vulture by 2008. With no vultures to eat them, the rotting carcasses of millions of cows oozed putrefaction into the environment. Dogs hied to the gamey feast, their numbers exploded, and rabies followed with them.

Rationalists, I imagine, will be relishing a familiar ire at this point, noting how a religious taboo against snuffing cows leads inadvertently to thousands of agonized human deaths. Well, don't let your eyes roll out of your head just yet. It gets worse.

In a country with more rabies deaths than any other in the world, where the disease has been known for some 3,000 years, you would think that even the most uneducated people would have a healthy fear of it. You would think that every nip and scratch from a strange dog would occasion a speedy trip to the clinic and a demand for a shot of vaccine (considerably evolved since Pasteur's day—no more bore needle, kids, more like a flu shot). Instead, tens of thousands of rural villagers, especially in west Bengal, are as likely to repair to a *bara ojha*, a witch doctor, who judiciously pronounces them pregnant with *puppies*.

Go ahead and read that again if you like.

"Puppy pregnancy syndrome" is a psychosomatic illness and form of mass hysteria whereby a person is convinced that they are knocked up with a litter of pups. Often they are scared off conventional medical treatment, as this would interfere with the witch doctor's magical cures. While either sex may become "pregnant," men have an additional reason for concern, as a man's puppies will invariably spring from his penis. It is worth noting that the afflicted often say they are able to *see the puppies* when they look at water, indicating some shadowy awareness of the real danger—rabid hydrophobia.

Science. Reason. Enlightenment. Ho.

Up the hill from the Tsuglag Khang, where the long vista of deodar hills gives way to shop fronts, and Indipop tangles with the sonorous Tibetan chants, I saw a dog I knew. "Bully Boy! You g'boy, you c'mere!" Tank-bodied, black and snow-slippered boss-dog of upper Temple Road, Bully Boy gave a snort of recognition and reared up.

The first time I'd seen this mighty heap I'd been in town for about a month, heading in to get some dinner after a day of teaching, walking down this very stretch. Dog screams reached my ears, and lo, there he was, at the center of his pack, persecuting some poor, runty little mutt, pinning him down in a gutter and snarling right in his ear, driving him to ecstatic terror. Some old shopkeepers and a few tourists were standing around, concerned but ineffectual. I walked by, walked about ten more paces and stopped. It was just so goddamned pathetic.

Dogs don't actually smell fear, but they are very good at reading it in your bearing, so the importance of believing in yourself cannot be overstated. I took a sip from my water bottle and settled my nerves. I walked over and splashed some water on the big dog, gave him a light kick in the haunches. The snubnosed howitzer head swiveled around and tracked me up and down. I snapped my fingers and pointed at the ground. "You c'mere!" I said in my best command voice. He did. I reached down to knuckle his meaty head, holding my breath. He stood for it, tongue lolling, and behind him his victim slipped away.

So I knew this old stinker; we had history. He was a priority target for our little roundup today, not only for the damage he could do if he ever went bad, but because his pack would see and follow his example. I called to him and he lumbered out into the road. He was halfway across when he noticed the five other green shirts closing in around him and realized something was up. He barked and retreated, dog-ass jacked low, tail whipping the dust. I took out a wad of meat and set it on the ground at my feet, called again, and he shuffled forward and back, growling and snorting, bluster and reticence tugging his heartstrings to a stamping, beastly dance. So went the negotiations. Finally, with extravagant humility, like some cannibal warlord receiving the Cross, he bowed to gobble up the treat and allowed Thukjay to move in. The needle darted the hide and all creation sang, for Bully Boy had allowed into his noble dogbody some cells distilled from purified chicken embryos hosting the attenuated rabies virus—*huzzah!* We touched him on the head with a dab of red paint, and Jamba blessed him in the name of Shiva, and we moved on.

Up the hill and down the stairs, through dank and gloomy alleys, in and out of shrines and noisome dump yards and ramshackle construction sites—where the dogs were, we went. We came coaxingly, petitioning with morsels of meat, slowly surrounding them. The catch pole was a last resort, as it usually sent the trapped one into a screaming frenzy that scared off every dog for a mile. Much better if they came willingly.

The trusting, meek, the sweet-faced little creatures were the easiest, and the big alphas like Bully Boy were not so difficult either—confident enough to come over and give us a sniff, take some meat and a shot. It was the middle-rank dogs that gave the most trouble. Cowardly heralds, they scampered and raised the alarm as soon as they saw us coming, scattering the packs. This was their role, their *raison d'être*. Nevertheless, the trick was to make every dog feel at ease, secure in the knowledge that he was basically a good boy, needing only to submit to the minor pain in order to stave off a great one. Inoculation against the madness, against a horror past all reckoning—that was what we were selling, and it helped to bear this in mind.

We'd covered a good portion of the town, and with the sun touching off the western clouds, we agreed to carry on in the morning and parted ways. I went to my apartment near the school and washed up, then headed back into town for a meal.

Coming up Temple Road I spotted a skinny teenager who always followed me around begging. Not today, kid. I stepped into an alley and came out on Jogiwara Road, waved to some Italian girls I knew from yoga class. I passed under the façade of Black Magic, the Indian-owned club I'd been avoiding since I'd heard the Tibetans were boycotting it. Apparently a couple of their men had gotten busted up in there. They'd been giving the owners a hard time, breaking bottles and such (Tibetan men have a reputation here as bad drinkers), and no surprise they'd caught an ass-kicking, but on top of that they'd been stripped, thrown in the street, and urinated on. Now that did seem over the top.

Even here, in Shangri-La, there was no shortage of trouble and ominous signs. That night, as I sat just inside the door of the Tibet Kitchen restaurant on the main square, eating an ice cream sundae in the cool blue evening light, I heard a man shouting in the street over a bullhorn. This wasn't unusual; it was a rowdy patch of turf, but I noticed the man was shouting in English.

"There is great darkness coming! None of us will escape it! We all must be prepared!"

I usually don't have time for cheap zealots spouting off about the end of days, but for some reason I took note of this one, even left my table and went over to the door and put an eye on him. He was an older Indian gentleman, normal-looking enough, not some red-eyed, naked sadhu. In fact, he looked a bit like my old philosophy teacher at Southern Oregon University.

I remembered reading that we are supposedly deep into the Kali Yug, the "Age of Kali" (a demon, not the goddess), the last in a series of cosmic eras that see the universe end in corruption and decay. After being purged in the fire of one thousand suns, the world will be reborn to a golden age of gods, but for now the bull of Dharma is barely standing. His three legs of austerity, cleanliness, and mercy have been broken by the demon, and his last good leg, truthfulness, is under enormous stress.

That night, like almost every other, I went to sleep with the howling of dogs in my ears. This is normal. The hills are crawling with them, and they call to each other, volley upon volley of fulsome dogsound seeking its answer, seeking itself, filling the vault of twilight high above the river.

Of course I dreamed of them that night—dogs. Or at least

the silhouettes of dogs—moving against an uncertain light, coming down a grassy hill with their noses to the ground and the wind combing the grass like fingers through dogfur and there was an electric tension in the air—a herd of dogs (strange because dogs are not herd animals), but . . . where was I? Shepherding them? Was I a dog myself? So I dreamed in the space between dog "Taps" and Tibetan "Reveille," awaking as usual to the sonorous bull-seal lowing of the dung-chens, the ten-foot ceremonial horns, aimed like cannons from the temple ramparts, calling me back to my work in the world.

Now, the dogs of Bhagsu Road were another breed of headache altogether, a shady, suspicious bunch, difficult to approach. They lived down a crowded strip of road, harried about by tuk-tuks and taxis and, surely, kicking pedestrians. I couldn't identify any clear alphas among them; they were just a loose gang, strung out along the road, gathering and scattering according to their jangled instincts.

Perhaps they were under the influence of Bhagsu Man, the blue-eyed old Pashtu ghoul who sold hash and opium from a concrete garret overlooking the street. Bhagsu Man was so brazen, so well-known, that I figured he had to be locally greased-in, a fixture, a demon counterweight to the Dalai Lama on the other side of town. I'd been to see Bhagsu Man once, on the dubious advice of friends, and I'd gotten such an ill vibe off the guy that even if the dope were free, I wouldn't have gone back. He remembered me, though, and grinned down at me from his deck as we threaded our way through the welter and snarl. I fingered my Shiva medallion through my shirt and looked ahead.

The sun was pressing a dense heat through the clouds that day as we scouted dogs in the rank and dusty byways. Again, I was impressed by their awareness of us and our mission. Many of the difficult ones, the slinkers and stinkers who took the most effort to bring under the needle, changed their attitude remarkably thereafter and followed us about, shriven and light-footed, as we worked to bring in the rest. But there were incorrigible, hard-core punks as well.

At one point I was ministering to a sweet, filthy little mop of a dog, and managed to slip her a shot, and she whined and whimpered in exquisite pain. "I know, I know," I said. "Doesn't hurt as bad as rabies though." Just then I looked back and saw a mid-sized, liver-ticked jackal yawning yellow fangs at my exposed calf. I shouted and swept my leg, and the would-be biter ran for cover. We come with reason, and mercy, and the best of intentions. Still there are those who only know to respect force, and for them, catch poles, *fucking catch poles for the wretched lot-taya, before you infect us all!*

At another point we veered off and worked our way down into the overgrown valley, where goats foraged in the refuse and clans of jabbering macaques mobbed the trees. Here was a complex of two-story brick flats where the most elder Tibetans lived, attended by nuns. They made a surreal audience, watching us from their porches and balconies, ancient faces without expression, eyes that had seen the Chinese overrun their homeland and commit the most atrocious crimes, now watching us give shots to dogs. The liveliest was an old, drunk crone who shuffled amongst dogs, berating and calling to them, swinging her cane at any she found insolent. Finally, one of the nuns came out and led her back inside.

We were helped immensely by the Tibetan womenfolk, who, beside their often angry and dissolute men, appear almost saintly in their compassion and fortitude. It was they who knew these dogs the best, and it was often their rapport alone that brought in the shy ones and the sly ones and spread the good work.

I contemplated this as we stood on a narrow staircase between a stone house and a steep gutter where giant horned slugs slipped and rolled and plopped in the stream that percolated through the moss. The snaggled, golden smile of the old lady in the doorway had the sunlight in it, and it bid the good creatures to come, and be not afraid, but take refuge from the terrible thing that stalked them. And I reflected that the overcoming of ignorance is secondary to the overcoming of fear, and the science in our needles and the benevolence of Avalokites'vara were not discreet forces here. The Buddha was in the pink serum and raw meat. Nor should we forget that Sarama, the goddess on whom Yama sired his deadly hounds, is also a goddess of the dawn, presaging human understanding. It is in the nature of this place that seeming contradictions are resolved into a complex dance, with nothing final, nothing fixed.

Today there is some cause for hope in India, at least on the rabies front. The veterinary version of diclofenac was taken off the market in 2001, and vaccination programs and public awareness campaigns are having an impact. But ignorance and evil are deviously resurgent. According to the World Health Organization, someone dies of rabies in India every thirty minutes, mostly children under fifteen (my old nightmares are their living reality). And that little boy that Pasteur saved? He died. He got to grow up and have a family first, which is no inconsiderable thing, but he also lived to see the Germans invade Paris. Believing, mistakenly, that his family had been killed in a bombing raid, he committed suicide by inhaling gas. Happy endings are hard to come by.

That day we made our way up to the next town, Bhagsu, and worked the precinct of the Shiva temple there. I had an afternoon class to teach, and I asked Thukjay if he could manage without me. He said he could, and I headed back towards Dharamsala. On the way down I came upon a distraught woman—Russian, by the sound of her—kneeling by the side of the road. She was holding a cardboard box, inside of which was a yellow cat. It had been hit by a car, apparently, and couldn't move its hind legs. The woman didn't speak much English, but she saw my green shirt with Tibet Charity Animal Sector on it and, mistaking me for a vet, pressed upon me the mission of saving the cat.

I accepted, reluctantly, and without much hope of a happy outcome, as the cat seemed done for. I thought about taking her to Bhagsu Man for a big dose of the poppy. Instead I flagged a tuk-tuk and brought the cat and box down to the school where, not knowing what else to do, I put her in one of the bathrooms and went to class. The next morning I hired a cab and took the cat down the hill to lower Dharamsala and a Tibetan-run animal clinic, where I wound up assisting with the suturing of another cat, which had been bitten by a dog. I left on the promise from the presiding vet that my cat would be taken care of. Then I went back up to the school and cleaned the bathroom.

There is indeed a darkness spreading in the world—who can deny it? And who can say if it's something new or just the ramifications of what always was. It is hydra-headed, constantly changing its angles of attack, and it forces us to adapt, to be just as clever and twice as tough. What we learn in simplicity as children, we must learn anew with each traumatic confrontation. Rationalism and science, religion and faith—have we not seen how each has its season, each its proper ebb and supplement? But while our strategies must evolve with the enemy, must be canny and varied, our stabilizing touchstones remain simple and pure.

Believe in yourself. Stand on truth. Be prepared. Now let it come.

FINALISTS

Sara Amis
Sara T. Baker
Cecilia Walker
Ben B. Walton

Clouds and Jupiter

Sara Amis

Part 1: Jupiter, 1994

I wasn't there when my son was born. I was there in body but not in memory, my ravens gone wandering. I was there, but all I have are fragments. I remember looking at the clock, silver rim and institutional black numbers. I remember being told I'd have to be put on a Pitocin drip, that my blood pressure was going up and up and it was dangerous.

July. Nineteen. Nineteen. Ninety-four. The breakup and impact of the Shumaker-Levy comet lasted several days. My son's birth lasted several days, at least from my point of view. In technical fact it was six hours of induced labor. Compressed labor. Quickly done, this sounds good, but it's not. If anything requires time, it's birth.

I remember when my son was born, when his head crowned. That part is very clear. The next thing I remember is him lying on my belly, looking away from me, dark and blue and the nurse saying he wasn't breathing.

Out in the orbit of Jupiter the object called Comet P/Shumaker-Levy 9 broke up into twenty-one distinct and individually tracked fragments and crashed into the upper atmosphere of the planet. Each caused a fireball and a plume, left gaping black holes in a line across Jupiter's agate stripes. On July 19, fragments K and L created impact sites in the banded clouds which were each at least an Earth-diameter across.

I don't remember anything after that. Electrical signals in my brain scrambled, I had a seizure, my blood pressure went up above what my body could take. My son spent the next few days in the intensive-care nursery. I was told that, later. I wasn't there. I was on Jupiter, with clouds full of explosions. I have said that I was holding the gates between the worlds open so that a great soul could pass through. I have said I don't remember. I was on Jupiter.

Eventually it seems I grew tired of being pieces of ice, being pulled apart by tidal forces and floating around until I hit atmosphere. The last thing I could remember from Earth was that my baby hadn't been breathing. I asked everyone, "Where is he? Bring him to me," but they wouldn't move him from the ICU. I'd fall back into outer space and then wake up again later, asking, "Where is my baby?" My mother-in-law told me that the nurses in the ICU thought he'd been abandoned because no one came to see him. For years I would go there in dreams, trying to make it up to him.

An infant's eyes are a dark gray-blue, slate color like limestone or thunder clouds. They look at you from somewhere else, still getting used to seeing. Freshly back from Jupiter, I found that my own body had become strange in my absence. I had spots in my vision. The pressure had caused tiny explosions in the blood vessels of the retina, irregular splotches one two three like the scorch marks in the Jovian atmosphere.

My three-day-old son and I understood each other very well, or so I think. At the time I was worried; did he think I'd forgotten about him? Had he forgotten about me? I held onto him as best I could, weak and with the itchy ache of plastic running into my body, and whispered in his ear, "It's me, it's me, it's me.

I didn't go anywhere. It's your mama. It's me."

A full week later I named him for the Raven of stories who sees beyond the world and brings back poetry and visions, trickster Raven who stole the sun and created life as we know it, twin ravens Hugin and Munin, thought and memory, who sit on the shoulders of Odin. I also named him Joseph after my father, who had died of a brain tumor the year before. I sat in the hospital room with my father for endless hours listening to him breathe, as ten years later I would sit with my mother. I thought my Raven could bring my memories back, or make new ones, like recording over old data.

I couldn't read or look at a computer screen for months, because of the explosions. I couldn't work. I didn't want to, much. Adjusting to Earth, and learning how to cope with my fellow new citizen, took up all of my time.

Part 2: Mix It Up With Your Hands, 1996-97

When the Olympics did come to Atlanta, my mother called me up. "Are you going? You should go." She meant that she wanted to go, but didn't feel up to it.

"I don't have that kind of money," is all I said. I worked at Underground Atlanta reading Tarot cards. The office job I'd had when I got pregnant was on another planet from the one where I lived, and so was being able to afford hundred-dollar tickets. Everything I liked was too far away or cost too much money, and why go and stand in line to see something I didn't care about just to say I'd been? It was all a giant nuisance. I didn't even make money off the Olympic tourists: They weren't interested in having their fortunes told.

Things improved a little after my husband got a job working

security at the Omni. But before too long I was hearing how stupid and incompetent the manager was, and not long after that Julian quit. He went to visit his mother in California and took Raven with him, while I stayed in Atlanta and paid the bills. I realized that I missed my toddler, but not my husband.

Home is where you go when you don't have anywhere else, so that's where I went.

You have to understand a few things about my mother. She graduated from the University of Georgia in 1943. There are old *Pandora*s in the library on the first floor where the reference desk is, behind and to the left. Mobley, Joyce. When you look at the picture, which is black and white, imagine you are looking at a woman with curly auburn-red hair and dark grey eyes.

She preferred English, but her mother and her school principal thought a degree in home economics was more practical. In those days people thought it was risky sending a woman to college at all, even a valedictorian who had skipped ahead two grades. "Why are you spending all that money to send Joyce to school? She won't do anything but get married," they would say to my grandmother. They never said it twice.

My mother cooked, as far as I can tell, exactly the way her own mother cooked, and hers and hers. Biscuits, cornbread, fried chicken, fried steak, fried catfish, okra, green beans with fatback, chicken and dumplings . . . all that. Middle Georgia farmer food, battered and fried, the kind that will raise your cholesterol if you stand too close to it.

The home economics degree did surface occasionally. My father planted a big garden and my mother canned and preserved what came out of it. I got to do plenty of picking but I was not involved in the canning and preserving. My mother was too impatient to stand there and watch me do anything. Even if she had something else to do, she would give a constant stream of advice and then take over. I learned early on that the way to actually get anything done in her kitchen was to ask how to do it first, then go in there while she was watching *The Wide World of Sports* or *Perry Mason* re-runs and cook. Usually I could get done before she came in to supervise. Sometimes my timing was off.

"Do you need any help?"

"No."

"All right. If you say so." My mother liked to drink ice water. She would get a glass and open up the freezer; it had metal handles and you had to be careful not to open the refrigerator and touch the metal cabinets at the same time or it would shock you. Also you had to jerk it open, and it made a loud *squnching* noise as the liner released. SQUNCH. Clink. Clink. Thump, the door closes. Water fills the glass with a rising tone. Pause. She looks at my row of measuring cups and spoons and a cookbook open. "Are you sure?"

"I'm *sure.*"

"You know I don't measure for biscuits. You just put the flour in and mix it up with your hands until it feels right."

"I *know*, Mama."

"All right," washing her hands of the consequences. "I'll be in the living room. Don't mess up my good pans."

I gave that remark the attention it deserved. My father, a former tech sergeant, required that I always respond with *Yes, sir,* or *No, sir*, but my mother didn't care. Her side of the family was altogether less uptight and Baptist. She called her own mother "Mother," or "Polly," and when Joyce was a girl during the Depression, she'd go out with her uncles to hunt and fish. They'd catch a big mess and hold a fish fry, and when they threw big parties they made their own music, sang, and *danced*. They were Presbyterians.

On Sundays our family went to the Baptist church for Sunday school, and then went home. I'm not sure whether that was meant to be a compromise or a comment on the preacher, but nobody ever stopped me from dancing.

My mother liked to take me shopping, but we had different ideas about what I should wear. At that time I was the only one in a three-county radius who knew who the Ramones were, and I single-handedly brought punk rock to Ringgold, Georgia. I got away with a lot of things because I was the first person to think of it, like showing up to school wearing a Hefty bag and a dog collar around my neck. That was when the dress code's possible infractions were limited to hot pants, see-through shirts, and offensive or obscene language. I was personally responsible for several additions.

When I went to college, Joyce thought I should be wearing skirts and sweaters, which is what *she* wore in college in the 40s. She would have put me in bobby socks and saddle oxfords if she could have found any. I shopped at the thrift store for old army jackets, plaid pants, and motorcycle boots. My mother asked, "Why don't you dress like a girl?" I started working for Greenpeace and bought ankle-length peasant skirts in bright colors, tie-dyes, loose cotton embroidered shirts from India, and braided hemp.

Her health began to fail. She was supposed to be on a diet; no more lard, no more fatback. No batter-fried anything. Whole grains, fruits, vegetables, skim milk, and only small amounts of doctor-approved vegetable oils, such as canola. Meanwhile I took to eating bean sprouts, brown rice, and spirulina.

By the time I moved back home after all my calamities, toddler in tow, I had developed very firm ideas about food. I read labels and rejected anything that sounded too industrial. Refined sugar had never crossed my three-year-old's lips.

My mother proceeded to feed my son cookies, candy, and ice cream whenever he asked for them. She'd say "That's what grandmothers are for." Then when he went galloping through the house like a two-foot rodeo, she'd say, "Why can't you control him?" I would start to do my laundry, and she'd tell me I was mixing my clothes wrong. I'd start to clean out drawers that hadn't been looked at in twenty years so I could put my belongings in them, and she'd say, "Are you throwing that away? I don't want that thrown away"; then she would complain about the clutter. I'd cook, and she'd come in the kitchen with suggestions. She wouldn't let me drive her car, and she bought only white bread because that was what my brother and the dog liked.

I was twenty-nine, and trapped. I picked violet leaves and plantain out of the yard and ate them in a salad. My mother wanted to know why I was eating weeds. I pitched a tent in the pasture and slept in it with my monkey-wiggle son. The pasture hadn't had a horse in it for twenty years and was more pine trees than grass, but it was at the farthest edge of the property away from the house.

"Why on earth do you want to sleep down there in the pine trees?"

"It's quiet."

One day my mother went to feed the outside cats and fell down the back steps. She broke her collar bone and had to wear a sling, blue canvas with white piping and adjustable straps made of that corrugated nylon stuff they put on gym-bag handles. She hated it. She was not allowed to cook, pick anything up, or drive. She was supposed to rest.

Suddenly, I had control of the household. I cleaned out the back bedroom so Raven and I could sleep in it, and snuck out the back door with the trash. I sorted my laundry as I saw fit. I put the cookies out of Raven's reach. I did all the grocery shopping, and I bought whole-wheat bread.

I surveyed her pantry shelf, which was full of things she bought because they were on her diet but never actually ate. I started working my way through them. I cleaned out a drawer in the kitchen and found the food list from her doctor in the bottom of it. I decided that I would cook only food from her diet. Oatmeal for breakfast and bran muffins for a healthy heart. Baked fish, steamed broccoli, and salads, all flavored with lemon juice and herbs.

My timing was off. *Murder, She Wrote* was over and my mother came in the kichen. "I don't like baked fish."

"Just wait. It'll be good."

She took the filet out of my hands, dipped it in corn meal, and fried it in canola oil, one handed. "You can cook yours any way you want. I'm going to fix mine the way I like it."

Part 3: Walking the Labyrinth, 2003

Labyrinths are older than written language. A true labyrinth, like the medieval eleven-circuit labyrinth at Chartres Cathedral, has one single path that curves inward and then leads you back out. This is a form of spiritual progress, a pilgrimage contained in eleven winding turns that bring you back to where you started.

I am on the phone with my mother. Her conversation winds back on itself. She knows it, but she can't seem to find her way out. There is a labyrinth on the floor of my living room, marked out on the carpet with baking soda. I walk in towards the center and back out again, holding the phone to my ear. I look at my books. I look in the mirror. I go back into the labyrinth, and come out again.

"I can't do anything, I can't remember anything," Joyce says. "I wish I was dead." I have nothing I can say to this. I keep walking. My skin is being flayed away, very softly, muscle and tendon exposed to the air. I can't feel it at first, it only hurts afterward, when I hang up the phone. I can't bear this, this ordinary sadness, this thing that happens to everyone if they live long enough. What happens when it hits bone? I don't know yet.

The labyrinth of the minotaur was actually a maze. A maze can have many paths, most of which lead nowhere. A maze, therefore, is a place where you can get lost. The most ancient seven-circuit Cretan form of the labyrinth looks somewhat like a human brain when seen in cross-section from the side. The brain, however, has billions of pathways created by the cross-connections of neurons, all of which are supposed to lead somewhere.

A few years before I made the labyrinth in my living room, I moved to Chicago briefly. The job I moved for turned out to be a chimera–an illusion with a nasty bite–but while I was there I went to a labyrinth ritual. When we came to the entrance we were challenged, given a flower and a tiny bag of seeds, and asked, "Who are you?" At the center of the twisting path there was a man wearing a bull mask. He held up a mirror and said, "Know the source of your fears."

St. Philip's Cathedral in Atlanta has a labyrinth, as do the Unity Church and St. Gregory the Great Episcopal Church in Athens, Georgia. All of these are eleven-circuit Chartres-style labyrinths. In medieval Europe, pilgrims sometimes traveled for the sake of another. I don't know how they did this. I imagine them taking some token to the holy shrine, and bringing it back.

I hold the phone to my ear, and I walk.

I have a labyrinth in my living room, but in the hospital where my mother eventually goes, they do not have a labyrinth. I go there too, and wander the halls, getting lost on my way to the cafeteria. The hospital is a maze. My aunt Gayle gets lost. My sister doesn't. She already knows her way around.

"Please," my mother says, "please, please, please."

Palilalia. It's a medical term, one of those Latin words they use to dance around what they're talking about. It means my mother says one word over and over and over again for hours and hours as I sit with her here in this hospital room, and the one word that she says over and over is, "Please . . . . Please. Please."

I have never before in my life heard my mother beg.

There is a labyrinth by the side of US 441 going north towards Rabun Gap, and one at a place called Starbridge in Dahlonega. A woman named Marguerite who lives down the street from me in Athens has one in her front yard. These are all seven-circuit labyrinths, like mine. When I go to the beach I like to draw a labyrinth in the sand as the tide goes out. It stays until the tide comes back. Sometimes I am the only person who walks it, but not always. Sometimes I come back later and find shells in the center that I didn't put there.

My mother climbed to the top of a thorn tree when she was twelve years old, just because somebody told her she couldn't do it. She was a Taurus, born in May, and true to the zodiac of Babylon she has always been bull-headed.

"Please," she says, "please."

My mother is lost in the labyrinth of the twisting crevices of misfired synapses and it's dark in there and I can't lead her out with string or blood or bread crumbs or a zodiac or love or stone patience. No matter how long I sit here and hold her hand, my mother keeps going away from me.

When she says anything else, it's random, like a radio dial cutting across stations and static. "I have to take my children with me," she says. "I don't have but two." She is somewhere in 1948, before my brother Jett was born. I won't be born for another twenty years, and I can't reach her.

Jett calls from Texas. He says, "I'm glad you're there with her. I don't think I could stand it." I hang up the phone, and think, I can't stand it. When do I get to stop this and get my mother back?

Later, Joyce notices me. She doesn't say my name, but I know she recognizes me. She tries to talk me into taking her home, out of the hospital. "You don't have to tell anybody," she says.

My sister Cathy was here when I got here. She sits with us and about eleven o'clock at night she asks me, "How can you do this without crying?" I don't answer. The only way I can do it is if I don't think about it too much. Speaking is thinking, and if I speak, I break the spell. So I sit and hold my mother's hand, which is the exact size and shape of mine.

The journey of the labyrinth is one of death and rebirth. *Resurgens.* Turn inward towards the center, spiral back out. Start again. However you move through the labyrinth, it remains what it is. My aunt, her sister, says Joyce doesn't know what she's saying, but I have been sitting here for a long time and I think she does. My mother is still in there. Every once in a while, around a corner, I can see her.

I sit with her all day, and sleep on a cot in the room at night so my sister can go home to her children. I tell the nurse when my mother is in pain, because she can't. My sister and the nurse say that she eats more when I am there.

Eventually, I am going to have to leave.

Cathy talks to Joyce the way you do when you don't expect an answer. I don't say anything. Cathy turns her back and walks out in case our mother still recognizes tears. Joyce looks at me, her eyes sharp and bright like a radio signal suddenly coming clear. She says, "Get me out of here."

Solomon and Hilda Are Dead; Long Live Solomon and Hilda!

Sara T. Baker

Solomon and Hilda must be gone now, I thought with a pang, adding up the years. Solomon had seemed ancient, Hilda only slightly less so, when I lived with them in Boston in the early eighties. Solomon and Hilda! In my solipsistic youth I had let them go, let them slip away from me in my headlong rush towards this, my own life. Why, my husband and I must be approaching the ages they were then—how had it happened? Hilda and Solomon had seemed both old and eternal, unchanging—a sort of enduring shelter.

But that was because they had sheltered me. And I was a girl in need of sheltering.

I was twenty-two, just out of college, having fled the South and landed in Boston. I was unprepared to make my way in the world, but dead set on doing so, propelled by a great unhappiness. I had washed up with a group of missionary nuns who lived in an impoverished part of Jamaica Plain and had an extra room for rent. I settled in with them, writing poetry, and taking black and white photos when I wasn't working as a temp. I would get early-morning calls to go to this or that part of Boston to do clerical work or substitute teach or work in a factory. Each day, I dressed in the cold and slipped out of the house into the still-dark morning. It seemed enough that I could maintain myself this way, that I could be independent. I was like a girl in a fairytale completing each day's onerous task, believing it would all add up to something, someday.

My art photography was put to an abrupt halt one winter afternoon. While taking a photo of a bloom of rust on an abandoned car, I felt a shadow fall over me. I took my eye from the viewfinder. A large man suddenly loomed above me. He was pointing to my wrist and I thought he was asking the time. Then he let loose a string of "f-ing bitch, f-ing cunt" in a strangely hushed voice as he grabbed the camera strap and twisted it around my neck. I went limp. He relieved me of my camera and camera bag, the camera and lenses gifts from my father. He pulled off my gloves, looking for a diamond ring, glaring at me when I turned out to be ringless and watchless. As he backed away, he told me not to scream, muttering that he was watching me, that he knew where I lived. Mute, I stayed rooted to the spot for a long time before finding I could move.

For weeks afterwards, I was unable to let anyone get physically close to me without panicking. On the Orange Line, my breath would grow shallow, my stomach clench as people pressed closer. That invisible psychic buffer I never knew I had was gone.

I had a friend, Tom, a gentle young man I had met months before when we'd gotten off at the same subway stop and he'd commented on my copy of *Seven Storey Mountain*. Skinny Tom, swathed in a wool muffler, a watchman's cap on his head, with frameless glasses that magnified his doleful brown eyes, reminded me of Lara's Bolshevik husband in *Doctor Zhivago*. He had that same pale otherworldliness. We walked all the way to the nuns' house that first day and stood by its chain-link fence, talking in the meager afternoon light. The mutt next door snarled and barked as we talked about books and ideas. Tom's round lenses flashed. What books? What ideas? Who knows? We were young, and passionate in our bookish ways. Now, alarmed at my funk, Tom invited me to a party at the house where he boarded. I hesitated, still spooked, unsure if I could handle a party. The thought, though, of watching Lawrence Welk with Sister Mary Martha was so dispiriting I overcame my reluctance.

Tom walked me over the night of the party. The house was in a more gentrified part of Jamaica Plain. Just a few blocks away, the large Victorian house sat on a small hill, sheltered by giant, shaggy, snow-covered cedars. Lit from inside, the interior rooms glowed, the light from them spilling out onto the blue-white snow. Tom opened the heavy wooden door, and I was ushered into a foyer papered in a lush William Morris floral, a thick red Persian carpet underfoot. I looked up at the sweeping staircase and around at the large pocket doors and gleaming wood floors. Laughter and music spilled from the next room; I could smell the fire in the fireplace. I was dazzled. Here was the exact template of my dreams. After so much sensory deprivation—the nuns' cold house with its gray linoleum floors, the subway cars with their odor of urine and the crush of stale bodies, the unrelenting diet of pizza and peanut butter sandwiches—I felt as if I were thawing, coming alive again.

Tom introduced me to Alex, the owner of the house, a slight, middle-aged, bespeckled man, rumpled in corduroys and a tweed jacket. He might have smelled of pipe tobacco, or that may be memory's ornamentation. He was different from what I expected. He had a recessive quality, but was kind, and soon had me talking about poetry and Yeats. He had a wife, a blonde Valykrie, who was hugely pregnant, and children that ran willy-nilly through the guests. I regaled him with what I hoped were amusing stories about my life as a temp. Alex must have taken in the whole picture—my haplessness and naïveté, my lack of carapace. On the spot, he offered me a job at the Board of Education as a "consultant." I remember great relief, but I am not sure I was surprised. Here was the fairytale's unexpected boon.

The job he gave me paid more than I'd ever been paid in my life and looked good on paper. It felt like a step up. It was weeks before I realized I was doing nothing more than glorified clerical work. In my innocence, I was shocked at how language was distorted to create bureaucratic opacity. I was appalled at the mind-numbing drudgery of office work, at the dispiriting gray cubicles, and at the petty office intrigues. I couldn't believe that shuffling paper could be called work. I actually liked factory work better, liked the banter of the Southies who worked at Gillette Foamy. But on the other hand, I liked knowing where I was going every day, and getting a salary. I understood that Alex had the beautiful house because he had traded his love of Yeats for the security of this job. I was beginning to see how the world worked.

Hilda was the head secretary in the office. She commanded a warren of desks for the secretarial staff. I had seen and heard her around the office. She was tall with a large squarish torso and an oblong head covered with black and gray hair in a severe bowl cut. She wore bright shirts in purple or pink hibiscus prints over slacks, as if she were on a perpetual vacation in Florida, and her raucous laugh frequently pierced the dull rat-tat-tat white noise of the office. I think my first encounter with her was when I needed aspirin for menstrual cramps and someone said, "Go ask Hilda."

Hilda, like Alex, must have taken one look at me and seen me for what I was. She clucked and challenged and teased me about my feckless state. She made fun of me to the other secretaries: "What are we going to do with this girl?" she'd say, so that I'd turn red, my feeble impersonation of an adult unmasked. She wasn't fooled by my love of Yeats or Merton; she wanted to know what my plans were, why I was living in a slum, why I was sick all the time, and if I had a boyfriend. She even sometimes brought me chicken soup. I protested that I could take care of myself, but I soaked up her fussing.

I was, however, becoming increasingly restless and disillusioned with the job. I no longer wrote poetry or read, my mind used up by the endless filling of forms. Tom studied theology at Boston College and took me around to look at it, urging me to apply. I liked the thought of spending a few more years reading and writing while postponing real life. So in my freezing attic room I prepared for the GRE, struggling painfully through the math and spatial problems. I squeaked by, and to my amazement, was accepted into the masters program in English. I resigned from the Board of Education. Hilda was delighted. She and Solomon lived in Chestnut Hill, right next to BC. I could rent their extra room. It was perfect—no more long subway rides, no more late nights walking past bars or drunks. And lots of chicken soup. I moved in that fall.

The house was a modest red brick one-story house. The front door opened onto a formal living room with a plush velvet sofa, loud floral cushions, and windows covered in lace and brocade. No one ever sat in that dim room. My room, off of the living room, must have originally been a sun porch. It was filled with filing cabinets, boxes of papers, odds and ends, and shoved into the middle was a bed. It may have been crowded and dusty, but it was mine.

All the real action in the house took place in the kitchen. Solomon, Hilda's husband, was as slight and quiet as Hilda was large and noisy. Gaunt, bald, and leathery, he seemed always to be sitting at the kitchen table, hunched over pieces of leather that he worked assiduously with his small metal tools, his glasses threatening to slip off the end of his nose. It wasn't a large kitchen, and Hilda worked around him, kvetching at every opportunity. He showed me his strip of leather: "Vat I used to do," he mumbled. His accent was very thick; I couldn't tell what it was, German or Hungarian or Polish. I never thought to ask, too involved in the drama of my own life. I think now that Hilda was lonely with her quiet husband. She made a lot of noise, banging her pans, muttering under her breath.

And so we passed that winter. I was happy in my new routine, working hard, and so surprised when I lifted my head from Cervantes one day and saw the first signs of spring. Spring in Boston comes slowly, tentatively, and each inroad made—a daffodil, snow melting off a roof, sunlight penetrating dusty southern windows—feels like a slow war being waged, one battle at a time. The sweaters come off, and the days lengthen. Still, when Solomon asked me one day, "Sarrahh, do you vant to go to the bitch?" I had no idea what he was talking about. Mutely, I stared at him. We were in the kitchen, as always, and Hilda laughed, turning from whatever pot she was stirring to explain to me that he meant "beach." His "beach" was the south side of the house, where he had placed two plastic lounge chairs facing the sun.

Of course I said yes. He was delighted.

Solomon and I trooped down through the dark basement to the outer door. He settled himself in one of the chairs, stretching out and sighing contentedly, as if this were the finest pleasure afforded a man. I was freezing. I turned my face towards the sun and hugged my sweater tight. Then Solomon took off his shirt so that he was in his sleeveless undershirt. "Have to get my beauty tan," he winked at me and closed his eyes again, a big grin on his face. It was only then that I saw the inked numbers on his inner forearm.

I stared. Suddenly, I was back in junior high, films of concentration camps and skeletal bodies flickering by as we sat dumbstruck in our hard chairs. The shock of those films had never left me. Solomon had come through *that*? The Holocaust seemed to have happened so long ago, yet here he was. My sense of history underwent a seismic revision. I wanted to ask him about those numbers, but when he opened his eyes again after a long time, I said nothing.

As Passover approached, in between writing papers on Faulkner and Henry James, I helped Hilda with her cleaning and cooking. The oldest of six children, I was competent when it came to domestic chores. "You would make such a good Jewish wife," Hilda said, shaking her head. "What a waste." Their daughter, a social worker five years older than I was, came around infrequently. I could see that being their only child was a big job. They were constantly grilling her about getting married, and they disapproved of her living with her boyfriend. Hilda could not resist bringing up her non-existent grandchildren. I recognized the daughter's need to keep some distance. Whenever our paths crossed, she regarded me with the clearly sardonic expression of the old soldier towards the young recruit. When I think of her, I always see her leaving, running down the steps of the house with her long black hair flapping behind her like a flag in retreat.

They didn't like my boyfriend either, and for good reason. I'd become entangled with an older man. It wasn't good and I knew it. Yet it was as if I were in his thrall. He had sniffed out my primal wound, the same wound Hilda tried to salve with chicken soup. I was sure I was unlovable. I thought enduring his abuse was the test of love.

One day when I came home late, Hilda asked to talk with me. Standing in the middle of the sacred living room, framed by brocade and lace, she said she and Solomon were worried about me, about this man. "He is not for you," she said, her dark eyebrows pinched together. Solomon stood beside her, reiterating everything she said in his heavy accent, like some sort of Eastern European echo chamber. I told them I appreciated their concern but that I could handle the situation. I went into my room and closed the door. Tears of shame and anger washed over me. I didn't want to admit the truth of what they said. I was an adult, after all. They were just old-fashioned. They really, really needed to stay out of my business.

Hilda never mentioned my boyfriend again, but I found myself invited that summer to parties with their daughter and her friends. Hilda worked behind the scenes, as would any good Jewish mother worth her salt. One of the daughter's friends took me on a few dates, and then one day offered to set me up as his mistress, since he couldn't marry a non-Jew. I didn't even like him, had only been going out with him to mollify Hilda. Horrified, I slammed out of the car and ran up the steps, catching a glimpse of Hilda behind the curtains. I wanted to tell her that her daughter's friends were creeps, even if they were good Jewish boys, but of course I never did.

I did break up with my alcoholic boyfriend. I like to believe I would have left him without Hilda's urgings, but I wonder now if I would have. Hilda was more right than she knew—his next girlfriend was found dead in her car of an overdose, and it was never determined whether it was suicide or an accident. Learning of her death was like waking from a dream. If I had stayed with him, would it have been me? We had been dancing close to the edge of an abyss.

It was winter again all too soon. Every afternoon I packed up my Selectric in its cumbersome plastic case and slogged through the snow to the library to work on my thesis. It seemed that it was always dark walking to the library, dark and snowy with a biting wind that went right through my thin jacket. I was doing research on a little-known female novelist whose name I no longer remember. What I do remember is how hard her life had seemed, how she had used her own unhappiness in her work, and how her work had been neglected by history. I liked her work, but can remember thinking glumly that someday some poor graduate student might stumble upon my scribblings and write a thesis about how I also just missed the mark. My mind then had a dark cast.

One day, walking to the library, I slipped on ice and sprained my ankle. After that, Solomon insisted on driving me to the library. My sprain healed soon enough and I began walking to school again, despite Solomon's protests that he didn't mind taking me, that he worried I'd hurt myself again. I was anxious not to have them hover over me or treat me like an invalid. I didn't want them waiting around for me. I felt like an adolescent, desperate to get out of the house, to be free, to meet my friends without a schedule, to be responsible only to myself.

One night, after a group study session, several of us decided to get Chinese down at Cleveland Circle. We walked outside into a blizzard. The sky poured endless snow; snow swirled violently under the street lights, and suddenly giddy, we found ourselves pelting each other with snowballs. Breathless with exertion, exhilarated by the cold and then the warmth of the restaurant, we dropped all talk of French deconstructionists and the work of William Burroughs. When I think of how ponderous we were at so young an age, at how we took ourselves so seriously! My head was full of Bachelard and Barth, of Gadamer and Pynchon, although even then I wondered what on earth any of it meant, really, for me.

I remember how that night, our faces flushed, we ate our

steaming sweet and sour soup and talked about our futures. One friend was anxious to meet a Holy Cross boy and get married and have babies; another was planning on law school. One already had worked out the minimum salary she would need to support her lifestyle. They were girls from a good Boston suburb, and this was their interlude before taking up their safe, prescribed roles. I couldn't articulate what I wanted, what my plan was. I felt passionately about so many things, and yet I didn't know how to translate that passion into a life. "I am going to take photos of plums in a glass bowl," I said, and as soon as I said it, realized how ridiculous and pretentious I sounded. I remember them laughing, someone saying, "You are content with so little." But that wasn't it at all.

It might have occurred to me as we ordered our next rounds of beer and pupu platters to call Hilda and Solomon and tell them I would be late. It might have, or I might have been having so much fun that they never crossed my mind.

We left the restaurant and began walking back up the hill. The snowstorm had not abated; if anything it had grown stronger, shrouding the buildings and trees so that we could barely see where we were. I remember how I loved it, loved how everything was muffled, indeterminate. Then, out of the corner of my eye I registered Solomon's old mustard-colored Chevy emerging from the curtain of white to come alongside us. My heart dropped. I slowed, and then stopped. My friends in front of me turned to look, puzzled. The streetlight gleamed on his bald head as he leaned over and cranked the passenger window down. "You gulls need a ride?" he said, looking at my friends.

"No, thanks," they said, while I reluctantly got into the car, mortified.

Solomon pushed the gas peddle and the car jerked and huffed into traffic. The humidity I'd brought with me fogged the windows. He looked straight ahead, driving with great concentration. Up close, I could see how deep the lines mapping his tan face were. Finally, he said, "Do you know vat time it is? Ve vere so vorried about you, Sarrahh. I've been looking for you for an hour." He turned to me, and I could see he wasn't really angry, just deeply worried. I sank down in the seat, ashamed of myself and yet irritated that my night out had come to an abrupt end.

"I am so sorry, Solomon," I said, and I meant it. I hated that he had been out in a blizzard searching for me. I hated that I had caused him anguish. Looking out the foggy window, I realized it was time for me to go.

I moved out that spring. I never told them what they meant to me, because I didn't know.

Going Home

Cecilia Walker

Swimming through the humid morning air, I stroll up the sidewalk of Jackson Street in wedges and pearls with extra time to kill before my history class. On this, my second trip of the morning, I am pleased to find that this time the gate of the Jackson Street Cemetery is slightly ajar. I cannot help but smirk at the little chain swinging as I carefully step on the dew-covered lawn. How funny to think that all of the dead in this small space should be jailed away from the outside world with a single lock and chain. Within the early morning peace, the cracked, eroded stones are loud and proud memories beckoning to me through the delicate silence of the cemetery. No, I realize. The dead are not locked in; the living are locked out. I smirk at yet another irony. How funny it is that the ghosts of our deceased, those whom we shriek at in haunted houses and scare others with in campfire stories, must fear the destruction of the living. My smirk melts off. The very thought of how others make such a sacred place scary sickens me. I stride out of the courtyard in the direction of my next class, closing the gate behind me.

Upon hearing of my macabre adventures, my four new roommates give me wide eyes and silence. Looking back, I don't blame them. It is probably hard to believe that the drawling, 105-pound little girl on the Pepto-Bismol-decorated side of the room enjoys reading time-weathered tombstones in abandoned graveyards. How could someone so seemingly bright and cheery have a fascination with dead people? Who dresses up for those buried too far down to see? So, who are you? Elle Woods or Wednesday Addams?

Normally, I wouldn't have given a second thought to such natural responses to my quirks. Yet, as I started a new chapter of my life at the University of Georgia, not even I could entirely dismiss this looming mystery: What am I? From choosing buses to choosing majors, the question of what I am demanded attention as I laid out my path for the next four years. But rather than tackle the uncertainty, I relied on my father's wisdom: the only certainty is in the results of hard work.

Channeling my fears and doubts into my academic efforts, I was certain that the person I would be in just a few years would have a 4.0 GPA and a résumé filled with extracurricular activity. And, thus, an incredible first year of new friends, good grades, and Insomnia cookies flew by without me ever getting closer to discovering who I was or wanted to be until it was all too late, with spring finals not even a month away.

After class on one of the last Fridays of the school year, running on what was left of my coffee, I took my homework and a hamper of dirty laundry into my car. Lunch-hour traffic turned my little SUV heading down Broad Street into a racecar on the Daytona 500. White knuckles molded onto the wheel, I swerve past angry minivans and roaring four-wheel drives, most with Cobb or Gwinnet county tags. As a relatively new Athenian, I quickly learned that blinkers and red lights are more like suggestions than rules. As I pass over the Clarke County line, my shoulders relax, and I let my tense back fall into the seat. My tired sigh sounds like a scream inside the silence of the car. It's unlike me not to have the radio on, but I hesitate to turn it on during that long ride to the middle of nowhere, not wanting to drown out this new silence or my old thoughts.

The summer prior to college, I had questions. Where is my home? What is my home? I know where my mail is delivered, and I know where my car will be parked at the end of this drive. And yet, back then, I had held my heart in my head, not convinced it would be safe in the county I worked so hard to leave.

While I wrestle with these thoughts of home, I unconsciously slow my speed from rush to casual cruise to only gas-the-pedal-to-average-speed after five other cars pass me. It was a struggle just to keep the speedometer up to the limit as I eyed bale after bale of hay, dotting the rolling fields.

With Monday only a few days away, I try to put my focus back on more important thoughts: the tests next week in economics; the applications to fill out for scholarships; the clubs I should join next year; the internships for a semester in Washington, D.C., I should apply for; the LSAT books I should already be buying. But the winding road dips into the pine forest, and I am lost again to the light that filters through the fresh green leaves and onto the creek cutting into the red gulley. Driving the car past the creek is like pulling a Labrador on a leash away from a swimming pool.

Despite the simple beauty of the land, I know the cold truth that lies beneath the sunlit fields. As the farmer's daughter, I see in the sea of green not only a good crop, but also a demanding thief, stealing weeks, months, and even years of life away from the farmer and a father away from his children. Down the tree-tunneled dirt roads that branch off the dusty pavement, I see not only the quaint simplicity of life on little front porches, but also the fear in a life in isolation, thirty minutes from the police department and an hour away from the nearest hospital. On this road that I know like my own reflection, I see all the things I do not want to be.

Continuing down the straight shot to my house, I pass a little white church barely hanging on to its stained glass windows. With no one else on the open road, I slow to a crawl as I inspect the adjoining cemetery to daydream of what mayor or soldier, writer or businessman lay forgotten beneath the weeds.

When just minutes away from my destination, I speed up around a bend before abruptly braking behind a car practically riding the back of a tractor. Of course, I don't enjoy creeping forty-five miles under the speed limit, but the old man riding in the heat on the open-top John Deere has no other option. However, the driver of the car in front of me thinks otherwise. Honking his horn, he swerves all over the lane, seeking a chance to pass on the curving road. My knuckles pop. I grip the wheel like a baseball bat, ready to knock out the jerk's taillights. A few more long honks later, the old man pulls the tractor down a side road, and the car whips off before the tractor is even off the pavement. Half of me wants to show the driver just exactly how I feel about him, but the other half wants to watch the farmer. So I stare at the farmer who works until the sun sets, the farmer who puts up with those who neither understand nor care to understand, the farmer who does the job nobody wants to do but everybody needs, the farmer who could have been my dad.

Making a left turn at the end of my road, my anger melts into sadness as my eyes water at a realization. For a whole year, I denied that the world I had spent eighteen years in was ever a part of who I am. I had believed that to succeed in corporate life, I had to leave my rural life behind. From my cemetery strolls and rodeo trips to my accent and cowboy boots, every part of who I am I carried with me for a year as I looked to be someone I thought was better, but here I was, no better than the jerk honking behind the tractor.

Swerving to avoid the potholes that are like land mines in the road, I try to compose myself before I reach the county line where the family farm awaits me. I look at the same barns, the same cows, the same trees, the same chicken houses, and the same road I grew up on with new eyes. In particular, I notice the lone massive tree that has towered in the middle of a cow pasture for all the years of my life. Its thick roots plunging into the earth did not stop it from reaching the great blue sky; its roots allowed it to grow higher.

Finally, the red barn and antebellum house on the Wilkes County line appear at the bottom of the hill. As I pull in past the pecan trees of my driveway, I feel safe and sound. Not everything I set out to know this year was revealed to me. There is still a mystery as to what new adventures await as I continue following my dream of becoming a corporate lawyer. But this world here in Wilkes County will always be mine no matter where I go in life. I turn the key, step out of the car, and am greeted by a menagerie of dogs, cats, and goats. I am home.

Laos: The Secret War

Ben B. Walton

In 1971, while in the Army on a second tour in Vietnam, I was stationed at Marble Mountain, three miles south of Danang, and was in command of the 478th Aviation Company. We flew the CH-54 Skycrane, a heavy-lift helicopter that could carry up to 25,000 pounds on a 100-foot cable. We transported everything from ammunition, food, water, fuel, and artillery guns to bulldozers and damaged aircraft. During that time, I participated in a secret war in Laos, flying helicopters in support of the Central Intelligence Agency (CIA), and Royal Laotian Army. Their mission was to fight the North Vietnamese Army (NVA) and communist Pathet Lao military in Laos and disrupt movement of the enemy traveling down the Ho Chi Minh Trail. My co-pilot, crew chief, and I would fly a helicopter from Danang over to Udorn, Thailand, and coordinate with Air America for daily operations in Laos.

For a long time, I was unable to speak of the secret war, but after twenty-two long years, in 1997, a bill was read in Congress, recognizing that there had indeed been a secret war in Laos during the Vietnam War. Also, it was resolved to recognize and honor the Laotian Hmong tribesmen warriors, Royal Lao soldiers, US paramilitary, US military advisors, and American clandestine operators of that war. A memorial was erected in honor of their contributions to US air and ground efforts during the conflict. The Laos Memorial is located on the grounds of the Arlington National Cemetery between the John F. Kennedy eternal flame and the Tomb of The Unknown Soldier.

From 1964 to 1973, the US rained down on Laos what would become the largest bombing campaign in history. During this nine-year period, the Air Force dropped over 2.5 million tons of bombs on the small Southeast Asian country. While the American public was focused on the war in neighboring Vietnam, the US military was waging a devastating covert campaign to cut off NVA supply lines through this small country, approximately the size of Utah. Laos is the most bombed country on earth, per person, in the history of warfare. Over 600,000 bombing runs dropped an average of one plane load of bombs on targets every eight minutes, twenty-four hours a day, for nine years— more than what American planes unloaded on Germany and Japan combined during World War II.

Unfortunately, the deadly legacy of the war lives on today in the form of unexploded cluster bombs, which had a 30 percent failure rate. Experts estimate that Laos is littered with as many as 75 million bomblets, which are baseball-sized bombs inside the cluster bombs. Since the bombing stopped four decades ago, tens of thousands of people have been injured or killed as a result. Laos, known as "The Land of a Million Elephants," is often referred to now as "The Land of a Million Bombs." An official US Air Force record of bombing activity over Indochina from 1964 to 1973 was declassified by President Clinton in 2000. That report gives details of the extent of the bombing of Cambodia and Laos.

In 2010, President Obama posthumously recognized Air Force Chief Master Sergeant Richard L. Etchberger for his courage under fire in 1968 during a mission on a remote Laotian mountain, a mission that was kept secret for decades because the United States was not supposed to have troops in the officially neutral Southeast Asian country. Etchberger was awarded the nation's highest military award, the Medal of Honor, after the government declassified his mission.

Most Americans don't have a clue about the secret war fought in Laos. If you were to ask where the country is located, most people would have no idea. A few may say, "I believe it's located somewhere in Southeast Asia." A few more would vaguely remember the Vietnam War and something about Laos being next to that country. For most people, though, there is little reason to know anything about Laos. For most of its existence, it has been a poor, quiet country, its people struggling daily just to survive. All that changed during the buildup and conduct of the Vietnam War. For some people during that time, Laos was of vital importance, and many people fought and died for control of the country.

The country is slightly smaller than Italy, but roughly the same size and shape. However, while Italy is surrounded on three sides by water, Laos is completely landlocked. The only large water feature is the Mekong River that flows south from China and acts as the border along the entire eastern side of the country, continuing into Cambodia and eventually emptying into the South China Sea. Laos is bordered on the north by Burma and China, to the east by Thailand, to the west by Vietnam, and to the south by Cambodia. In itself, Laos has little strategic importance. It is remote and landlocked, with a population of just a few million. However, it shares borders with these countries and has traditionally served as a buffer zone between these more powerful neighboring countries.

Laos existed for hundreds of years with warlords fighting for its territory and kings ruling the land. Around 1900, it became a French protectorate as part of French Indochina. It was occupied by the Japanese for a time during World War II, then returned to French rule after the war, but the country continued to experience a long civil war until 1975, when the communist Pathet Lao movement came into power.

In 1954, following the military loss at Dien Bien Phu, an international conference was held in Geneva to address the problem of Indochina. The conference produced ten documents called collectively "The Geneva Accords." The documents arranged a settlement that was supposed to end the fighting. A ceasefire was signed, and France agreed to withdraw its troops from the region. French Indochina was split into three countries: Laos, Cambodia, and Vietnam.

When Kennedy began his presidency in 1961, his first foreign policy crisis was not Berlin, Cuba, or Vietnam, but poverty-stricken Laos. Before his inauguration, Kennedy met with President Eisenhower, who told him that Laos lacked the ability to defend its recent independence. Its economy was undeveloped, its administrative capacity primitive, its population divided both ethnically and regionally, and its government disunited, corrupt, and unfit to lead. Eisenhower warned that this weak country was the "cork in the bottle" and its loss would be "the beginning of the loss of most of the Far East." His remarks prompted Kennedy to call for an end to hostilities and for negotiations leading to a neutralized and independent Laos.

An international agreement signed in Geneva in 1962 was a result of a conference between fourteen countries and Laos on settlement of the Laotian question. The fourteen signatories pledged to respect Laotian neutrality; to refrain from interference, direct or indirect, in the internal affairs of Laos; and to refrain from drawing Laos into military alliances and from establishing military bases in Laotian territory. However, the agreement was violated almost immediately when North Vietnam established a supply line through "neutral" Laotian territory for supplying military actions against the government of South Vietnam. More specifically, the NVA constructed and maintained the Ho Chi Minh Trail, which passed through the length of Laos. Thousands of Vietnamese troops were stationed in Laos to maintain the road network and provide for its security. NVA military personnel also fought beside the Pathet Lao in its struggle to overthrow Laos' neutralist government. The United States could not block the Ho Chi Minh Trail with ground forces because the countries it passed through were officially neutral. Undeniably, the trail lay at the heart of the war.

The year 1965 marked the beginning of major US military activity in what became known as the secret war in Laos. The CIA was largely responsible for conducting military operations, but the US ambassador stationed in Vientiane, the capital of Laos, was in charge. His orders were to maintain the façade that the Geneva Accords would be maintained and that there would be no US ground troops in Laos. The ambassador delegated responsibility for the tactical conduct of the war to his CIA station chief located next to Air America, an airline secretly owned by the CIA, in Udorn, Thailand.

Air America was a vital component of the CIA's operations in Laos from 1959 to 1974. By 1966, it had almost 6,000 employees and the largest airline fleet in the world in terms of aircraft owned, and it operated up to 30,000 flights per month by 1970. Air America airdropped or landed millions of pounds of food, mainly rice, transported tens of thousands of troops and refugees, flew emergency medevac missions, rescued downed airmen, inserted and extracted road-watch teams, flew nighttime airdrop missions over the Ho Chi Minh Trail, monitored sensors along infiltration routes, conducted a photo reconnaissance program, and engaged in numerous clandestine missions using night-vision glasses and state-of-the-art electronic equipment. Without Air America's presence, the CIA's effort in Laos could not have been sustained. Air America pilots were among the last to leave when Laos, Cambodia, and Vietnam collapsed. Over the years, many of their aircraft were shot down and lost, and 243 men were killed in action.

My co-pilot, crew chief, and I would begin the day in Udorn, visiting the Air America operations center and getting a mission and weather briefing. We would then meet our Air America escort pilots and load riggers and discuss the operations for the day. After that we would proceed to the flight line and begin our flight to Laos. Udorn is located only twenty-five miles south of the Laotian border, and in just a few minutes we would fly across the Mekong River that separates the two countries and be in Laos and in enemy territory. Vientiane would be just to the northwest as we crossed the Mekong. We would continue to fly north and gain altitude as we began to cross large mountains and rugged terrain. Eventually, we would cross over a mountain ridge and would see in the distance, sitting in a bowl surrounded by mountains, a town with a paved airstrip, and we would know that we were looking at Long Tieng, Lima Site 20A, "The Most Secret Place on Earth."

Until 1962, Long Tieng was a quiet little village with just a few inhabitants. But that changed when the CIA set up a headquarters for Hmong Major General Vang Pao in the Long Tieng valley. Within two years, a runway had been built, and by the late 60s the town had a population of over 40,000 people, and at the time it was second only to Vientiane in size. However, it never showed up on any maps during this period.

From the late 1950s until 1975, Long Tieng served as a town and airbase operated by the CIA. It was one of the largest US military installations on foreign soil and one of the busiest airports in the world. Located in a valley and surrounded by mountains on all sides, at an elevation of 3,100 feet, Long Tieng experienced many chilly nights and days of foggy weather. The "Secret City" had one paved road that ran through the town, and on both sides were tin shacks containing noodle stands, food markets, clothing shops, radio-repair shops, taxi services, and living quarters. The remainder of the town had unpaved roads, no sewers, no running water, and inadequate sanitation. At any time, you could see in the town American CIA personnel, Thai soldiers, South Vietnamese soldiers, and soldiers of the Royal Lao Military. The largest contingent was approximately 30,000 Hmong mountain-tribe soldiers commanded by General Pao.

(In 2008, German documentary filmmaker Marc Eberle released a documentary, *The Most Secret Place on Earth: The CIA's Covert War on Laos*. Eberle first got the idea to do the film when he visited the Plain of Jars in 2002. While there, he heard about Long Tieng and the fact that no one had been able to visit there since the war; the area still remained off limits to all foreigners and most Laotians due to continuing clashes with remnants of the CIA's Hmong Army.)

At Long Tieng, the Air America riggers would jump out of their aircraft and quickly hook us up to a load of supplies, and we would take off flying once more. Often, we would head northeast to resupply Royal Lao troops on the PDJ. The PDJ (from the French *Plain des Jarres*, or in English "Plain of Jars") is a 500-square-mile area located in north central Laos that became a highly strategic location during the Vietnam War. The PDJ gets its name from several hundred huge and ancient carved stone jars of various sizes that were discovered lying atop the plain. No one is entirely sure of their purpose, but it is thought that the jars served as burial crypts or funeral urns for high-ranking members of an ancient society, and excavations around the jars have supported this theory with the discovery of human remains, burial goods, and ceramics in and around the jars.

Situated near the Mekong River and the Ho Chi Minh Trail, the PDJ was a vital crossroads and staging area, and there was continuous fighting for its control between the NVA and local Pathet Lao units on one side and the Royal Laotian armed forces augmented by Hmong mountain tribesmen and Thai mercenaries and supported by the United States on the other. The PDJ has always been an important military strategic area. As far back as the 1200s, Genghis Kahn, the great Mongolian leader who had captured nearly all of Indonesia and China, stated, "Who controls the Plain of Jars controls Indochina."

During the long Southeast Asian war, all sides found the PDJ to be situated in a highly strategic location. The area was home to several airfields and contained a limited road complex that connected various sectors of Laos to the outside world. This crossroads has been a battleground for centuries, but never so intensively as in the twentieth century's many overlapping conflicts in Indochina. The PDJ was a sideshow to the main war in Vietnam, but it seems to me that it had some of the finest and most heroic flying in the history of the US Air Force.

The worst result of the struggle for the PDJ was the destruction of a noble ally, the Laotian hill people, the Hmong. They fought in countless battles against NVA forces and in the end were left to their fate. Originally numbering about 300,000 people, living on high mountain ridges and subsisting by means of slash-and-burn agricultural techniques, the Hmong suffered many thousands of casualties, mostly young fighting men. When the end came, those who could do so fled to camps in Thailand. A few Hmong relocated to the United States. Those who remained in Laos were for years hunted down and killed by

Laotian communists.

The intent of the Paris Peace Accords of 1973 was to establish peace in Vietnam and bring the war in Vietnam to an end, and Laos was supposedly provided for in the peace agreement. Both sides promised to respect the 1962 Geneva accords and withdraw their troops from Laos. As before, the United States stopped its bombing operations on schedule, and the NVA violated the truce. When the NVA moved into Saigon for their final victory in 1975, the Pathet Lao, supported by more than 50,000 NVA troops who were still in Laos, seized power.

Not much progress has occurred in Laos since the secret war ended. Officially, Laos is the Lao People's Democratic Republic. The country is a communist single-party socialist republic, dominated by military generals. With a population of seven million, a third of the population lives below the international poverty line. Outside the capital, many people live without electricity or access to basic facilities. Laos has one of the lowest annual incomes in the world and has a severe hunger problem. It also has a dismal human rights record, most particularly regarding the nation's acts of genocide being committed towards its Hmong population. Public dissent is dealt with harshly by the authorities. Laos relies heavily on foreign aid and investment, especially from Japan, China, and Vietnam. The country is also suffering from environmental problems, with deforestation a particular issue. Plans for commercial exploitation of the forests, as well as foreign demand for wild animals and other products for food and traditional medicines, put increasing pressure on the forests.

The future for Laos appears bleak. In some ways, after forty years, the war continues. There are over seventy-five million unexploded bomblets remaining, littering the rice fields, villages, school grounds, roads, and other populated areas. More than 34,000 people have been killed or injured by cluster munitions since the bombing ended in 1973, with close to 300 new casualties every year. Over forty per cent of the accidents result in death; sixty per cent of the victims are children.

So far, the United States has contributed an average of about three-million dollars a year to bomb-removal efforts. In contrast, the United States spent more than seventeen-million dollars a day dropping the bombs.